Father Day -
1973

Fond memories of our
Alaskan Trip

Rob

Every mountain he got Injun in it

Katahdin   he man

KATAHDIN'S WILDERNESS

Katahdin stands above the surrounding plain unique in grandeur and glory. The works of man are short-lived. Monuments decay, buildings crumble and wealth vanishes, but Katahdin in its massive grandeur will forever remain the mountain of the people of Maine. Throughout the ages it will stand as an inspiration to the men and women of this State.

Percival Proctor Baxter,
Portland Sunday *Telegram*,
November 30, 1941.

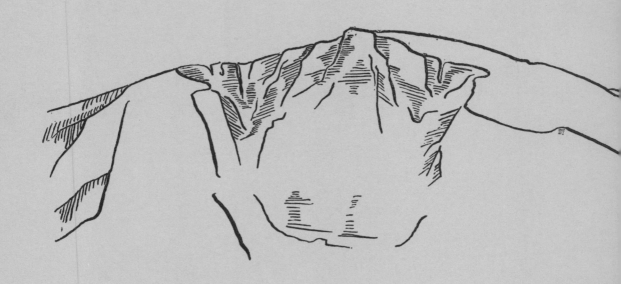

Mount Katahdin

Greatest Mountain:

Katahdin's Wilderness

Excerpts from
the writings of Percival Proctor Baxter
and photographs by his great grandniece,
Constance Baxter with a historical essay
by Judith A. and John W. Hakola

Scrimshaw Press 1972

Library of Congress Catalog Card Number 72-76270
ISBN 0-912020-25-3 *paper*, 0-912020-26-1 *cloth*

Publication number twelve by the Press
149 9th Street, San Francisco 94103

The endsheet quotations are from the oldest member of the
Penobscot tribe, as recorded in 1916, and appear in
"The Katahdin Legends," by Fannie Hardy Eckstorm,
Appalachia 16, December 1925

"Greatest Mountain" is a translation from the Penobscot
name for the mountain, Keght-Adene

The title page drawing (and the mushroom) are by
Nan O'Byrne, from an aerial photograph by Ryan Fendler

Dedicated to my father, whose backing and encouragement have allowed me to indulge in a photographic endeavor, and to my mother, who complements him beautifully.

C. B.

"Gigantic, majestic, with stony eyebrows and cheekbones, the Spirit of Katahdin lived inside the mountain with his Indian wife and his two children."

Katahdin, rising massive yet serene above the lakes and forests of northern Maine, has long exerted an almost magnetic attraction. For hundreds of years, the "greatest mountain" of the Abenaki Indians was honored as the dwelling place of their sacred spirits. In more recent times the mountain has lured geologists and botanists up its flanks, into its ravines, and among its subarctic or alpine meadows. Loggers of the nineteenth and early twentieth centuries could not resist the abundant softwood and hardwood on its lower slopes. For more than a century and a half, hikers of all degrees of competence have trudged, staggered, clambered, and otherwise got themselves as near to its summit as they could. A huge cairn at the top testifies to the success of many of them. Artists and photographers have always found the mountain a compelling subject. Whatever the medium, whatever the time of day or season of the year, it has challenged them to capture its spirit and appearance. Finally, Percival Baxter, son of a wealthy Maine family, found in Katahdin the gift he wished to give to the people of Maine. By the nature of his bequest, however, he presented them with more than a certain number of acres, more even than the highest peak in the state. By stipulating that the area "forever shall be held in its natural wild state . . . , " Baxter passed on his understanding of the need for wild places in the lives of all men. Today, as more and more of what once seemed an inexhaustable supply of wilderness is tamed and often utterly destroyed, the wisdom of Percival Baxter's gift becomes obvious.

How old is Katahdin? As Dabney Caldwell points out in his study of the geology of Baxter State Park, a complete answer must cover three points. First, the rocks which comprise the mountain are about 300 million years old. The bedrock is granite, grey at the lower and intermediate levels and pink at the higher ones, although lichen and weathering may obscure these colors. Like all granite, it is igneous, meaning that it was formed from a molten material. Because this particular granite probably cooled below the earth's surface, it is coarser-grained than the granite found on nearby South Turner Mountain. Katahdin granite was formed during the Devonian period, about the middle of the Paleozoic Era. Although 300 million year old rocks may seem ancient, there are three kinds of bedrock in Baxter Park which are older. The sedimentary rock underlying lowlands in the northern part of the Park is the oldest, formed at least partly when the area was covered by the oceans. Traveler Rhyolite, another igneous rock, underlies a large area north of Katahdin. And a small area of younger sedimentary rocks can be seen in the Trout Brook valley. It is the only rock in the Park containing fossils of land plants.

A second way of asking Katahdin's age is to ask how long it has had its present general shape. The answer is two to five million years. Before that it was undoubtedly higher, rougher, and with a sharper profile, much likethe western Rockies are today. But millions of years of erosion have worn Katahdin down.

A third answer to the question of age involves the specific features of Katahdin's landscape, such as the Knife-Edge, great and small basins, and its present altitude of 5,267 feet, all of which contribute so much to its fascination. Although Katahdin was covered by one or more continental glaciers (or ice sheets) during the various ice ages which have come and gone for the past million years, the distinctive features just mentioned were formed by the glacial action of comparatively small valley glaciers. Unlike the usual valley, which is V-shaped and narrow at its head, a glacial valley is U-shaped and widens into a bowl or basin at its head. This bowl is the cirque, and if the highland above the headwall of a cirque is narrow enough, glacial action will eventually produce another striking geologic feature, an arête. This is the narrow strip of rock which results when the glacier eats away at the headwall of its valley, until all that is left between it and the next valley is a ridge. The Knife-Edge and Hamlin Ridge were both formed in this way. Since the last period of glaciation reached its peak only about 9000 years ago, and since valley glaciers often remain active after continental glaciers have melted away, the answer to this third part of the question of age seems to be that Katahdin isn't very old at all.

Long before the first white men tried to climb Katahdin, the mountain had acquired an important place in the legends of the local

Abenaki Indian tribes. The earliest known record (in English) of these tales was made by John Gyles, an interpreter who was held captive by Indians from 1689 to 1698. By 1850, five other men had left reliable versions of these legends, usually taken directly from the Indians themselves. Not all stories that pass for Indian legends are authentic, however. In some cases, the mistakes are honest ones, the results of misunderstandings of both language and culture. In one instance, the Penobscots deliberately set out to hoodwink an Italian priest living in Old Town, whom they resented for his interference in a tribal quarrel. The priest's account of the Abenaki legends was reprinted many times, thus compounding his errors. Some of the more fanciful developed around campfires as Maine guides, entertaining hikers and other visitors in the Katahdin region, embellished the old legends or occasionally invented new ones. A few local writers, more interested in colorful prose than in authenticity, have carried on this practice.

A knowledgeable source of Katahdin legendry is the Maine author, Fannie Hardy Eckstorm (1881-1946). A lifelong acquaintance with the Penobscots and an intellegent, critical approach to the subject give considerable validity to her versions. Mrs. Eckstorm maintained that at least three different Indian concepts were covered by the Indian word *bumole* (the white man's *Pamola*). One was *Wuchowsen*, the spirit of the night wind, whom an old Indian woman described as having "no body, only leetle mite here [indicating her chest], all legs, hands." *Wuchowsen* created the breezes by flapping his wings and was considered harmless. A second was the Storm-bird, probably a variation on the Passamaquoddy and Maliseet *Culloo*. This was a huge bird-like creature, with fearsome beak and claws and a head as large as four horses. Some versions give him the head of a man while one modern sketch depicts a fanciful conglomeration — the lower half and the wings of a bird, the torso and arms of a man, and the head and rack of a moose. In his best mood this creature was nasty, and when aroused to anger — a frequent occurrence — he used his considerable power to create violent winds and devastating snowstorms. The third manifestation was entirely human in form. Gigantic, majestic, with stony eyebrows and cheekbones, the Spirit of Katahdin lived inside the mountain with his Indian wife and his two children.

The legends about the Storm-bird (usually designated as the Spirit of Pamola) concern his attempts to keep men from climbing Katahdin. As long as they stayed below the treeline, Indians and white men alike were safe from his wrath. Once they climbed higher, however, they

11

could expect no mercy. Many early writers about Katahdin mention Indian stories of braves who attempted to climb too high and disappeared completely. Gyles tells of three Indians who, after hiking for three and a half days, were struck by delirium. When their heads cleared, they found themselves near the foot of the mountain with no recollection of how they got there. Pamola used snowstorms, fog, and high winds to keep his mountaintop home free from intruders. In 1837, when Dr. Charles Jackson was attempting to calculate the height of Katahdin, a violent northeaster struck. The Indian guide with him declared that this was the work of Pamola, who was angry that someone had tried to measure his mountain.

The best-known legend concerns the adventure of the famous Penobscot chief, John Neptune, who went hunting on the mountain and spent the night there in a shack with a strong door. Pamola, enraged at Neptune's temerity, came swooping down from his stronghold to destroy him. He pounded on the door and blew and roared, but to no avail. The door was frozen shut. Pamola finally stormed away, and the next day Neptune descended the mountain safely.

Unlike the vicious Pamola, the Spirit of Katahdin showed a friendly concern for the Indians. The most frequently repeated story about him concerns his taking a bride. Several versions have been recorded, each with its unique features, but in essence the story is this. Once a young Indian maiden was gathering blueberries on the lower slopes of Mount Katahdin. As she looked at the mountain, she wished it were a man and would marry her. With this thought in mind, she lay down and fell asleep. When she awoke, the Spirit of Katahdin was standing before her. He carried her off to live with him inside the mountain, where she subsequently bore him a son and a daughter. Eventually she became homesick, so Katahdin sent her back with the children to visit her tribe. Before they left he granted the little boy, Katahdinosis, the power to kill whatever he pointed at. To the little girl went the strange ability to make come true whatever she said, if she first passed her fingers over her lips. When they arrived for the visit, they found the tribe in the grip of a dreadful famine. However, the boy and girl were able to provide food for all by using their magic gifts. When the boy pointed at ducks flying overhead, they fell from the sky. When he went out in a canoe and pointed at fish, the fish died and floated on the water where they could be gathered. When the girl passed her fingers over her lips and said the lakes were full of eels, they became full of eels.

12

In one version of the legend, the Indian wife stays on and helps her people defeat the Micmac Indians. Every hundred years she supposedly returns to visit her tribe. In another version, Katahdin told his wife she should forbid her people to question her about the boy's father. But the tribe cannot resist trying to discover who fathered this child with the magic gift. Finally, in exasperation, she tells them not only that the boy is the son of Katahdin, but also that they have lost the opportunity to have him lead them and make them a mighty tribe. Then she and the children go back to the mountain and never return.

The date when white men first saw Katahdin remains uncertain. Probably French and English trappers were familiar with it, although they left no written record of having seen it. The first mention of the mountain in print was made by John Gyles. In his account, Gyles mentions having passed near the mountain, which he calls "the Teddon," in a canoe. In 1760, Colonel John Montrésor, a British engineering officer who was exploring the area between Quebec and Moosehead Lake, indicates that he saw the mountain from a distance. The first known attempted ascent by a white man occurred in 1764, by John Chadwick, a surveyor, who climbed part way up the southern side and later drew the first map on which the mountain appears. It was another surveyor, Charles Turner Jr., who led a party in the first recorded complete ascent of Katahdin on August 13, 1804. They followed the Southwest Spur, now the general route of the Hunt Trail and the northernmost section of the Appalachian Trail. In fact, surveyors continued to be the primary explorers, for in 1819 the second recorded ascent was made by Colin Campbell, a British surveyor with the Maine Boundary Commission, which was surveying the boundary between Maine and New Brunswick. Another wave of surveyors arrived after 1820 when Maine separated from Massachusetts and more exact land measurements were needed.

During the 1830's, the first of many scientific expeditions to Katahdin were made. Professor Jacob Bailey, of West Point, and two faculty members from Waterville (Colby) College climbed the mountain in search of new material. They were followed shortly by the Rev. Joseph Blake, a botanist with a particular interest in arctic plants. Charles Jackson, the Maine State Geologist, ascended the mountain in 1837 during the course of the first Geological Survey of Maine. Because of its height and location, these men were able to gather data on Katahdin that was available to them nowhere else in the state.

Although scientific expeditions have continued to the present,

13

the 1840's saw the arrival of a number of climbers who were motivated as much by a sense of adventure as by scientific curiosity or professional necessity. In 1845, Edward Everett Hale and William F. Channing, then young Harvard students, attempted to climb Katahdin from the north, but were turned back by bad weather. Probably the best-known expedition occurred a year later, when a party led by Henry David Thoreau tried unsuccessfully to reach the top of the mountain by a route east of the Southwest (now Abol) Slide. Thoreau's account of his experience, published first in 1848, has intrigued thousands of readers the world over, and thus spread far and wide the name of the mountain. The Reverend Marcus Keep, a missionary in Aroostook County, made several ascents in the 1840's, and apparently was the first person to enter the Great Basin area. In 1848, he did a great service to hikers by clearing the first actual trail on the mountain. It led from the end of the road at Katahdin Lake to the Basin Ponds area, then up the East Slide onto what is now Keep Ridge, and up the Ridge to Pamola Peak.

Though climbing Katahdin was an arduous undertaking, especially before trails were marked and cleared, just getting to the mountain also demanded a good deal of planning and exertion. Most of the early expeditions followed the route of the West Branch of the Penobscot River. Even by the 1840's, however, there were at least thirty miles by water between the last inhabited outposts of lumbermen and the steeper part of the mountain near the Southwest Slide. Boats (usually batteaus) had to be poled or rowed up numerous rapids, around falls and dams, and across lakes and deadwaters before the final streams leading to the mountain itself were reached. The situation improved somewhat in the 1840's, when lumbermen began to eye the great stands of pine which covered the flanks of Katahdin in many places, as well as neighboring peaks and valleys. To gain access to the timber, a system of tote roads were built, although the logs themselves were floated out via the East Branch of the Penobscot and its tributaries. The approach to the mountain was from the east, from the so-called Aroostook Road (east of the East Branch) westward, first to the banks of the East Branch itself and then on to Wassataquoick Stream and Katahdin Lake. Although these roads were extremely rough and at best were fit only for buckboards, they did open up whole new areas to hikers interested in exploring Katahdin and attracted by its scenic grandeur.

The growing popularity of the Katahdin region with outdoorsmen was indicated by two developments in the latter part of the nineteenth century. First, a number of sporting camps were established on the lakes in the area, offering guests the opportunity to hunt, fish, and hike on the mountain. In fact, the popular Hunt Trail, which follows the Southwest Spur to the summit, was first carved out of the wilderness during this period by Irving Hunt, owner of one of the camps. Second, in 1887 the Appalachian Mountain Club, one of the oldest hiking clubs in the country, decided to send an expedition to Katahdin, partly as a result of intriguing reports written by two members, George Witherle of Castine, Maine, and Professor C. E. Hamlin, a botanist from Harvard. The importance of these two men in the thorough exploration of the mountain and subsequent publicizing of its glories is considerable. They rank with Marcus Keep and Thoreau as the major nineteenth-century figures in the history of the mountain. The expedition's base camp was at Chimney Pond, at the bottom of the huge glacial cirque known as the Great Basin. In preparation for the climb, club members relocated the old Keep Trail, which had become overgrown and was hardly usable. Thus one more approach to the summit was made available to the ever-increasing number of hikers.

As early as 1828, a group of surveyors had been sent to Katahdin by lumbering interests in the state. By the 1830's and '40's lumbering operations had started in earnest and were not to cease until the Great Northern Paper Company's last major operations of 1922 and 1923. By then nearly the whole mountain had been logged over, so that today there is very little virgin forest left. But long before lumbering activities were completed, advocates of conservation and preservation were beginning to suggest (about 1860) that the mountain be set aside as a state park or forest preserve. By the 1890's, a group of Bangor citizens were proposing the creation of a game preserve, and a Bangor newspaper suggested in 1895 that a thirty-mile square area surrounding Katahdin should become a state park. As the conservation movement reached its peak across the country, the idea of setting aside the Katahdin area as a National Park took hold. In 1916 a Maine congressman introduced a bill in Washington to this effect, but anxiety about the World War and lack of interest in the distant, unpopulated State of Maine combined to stop further action.

15

What the Katahdin park concept needed and eventually gained was a champion. The man who, in effect, singlehandedly created what is now Baxter State Park was Percival Proctor Baxter, son of a wealthy Portland businessman, longtime mayor of Portland, and leading Maine historian. Blessed with wealth, social standing and a good education (Bowdoin College and Harvard Law School), the young Baxter could have enjoyed a life of leisure, free from worry and responsibility. Instead he chose to involve himself politically in state affairs by running for the State House of Representatives. He served a two-year term beginning in 1905, then served a similar term in the State Senate. Baxter was elected to the House again in 1916 and 1918, and to the Senate once more in 1920. In 1921 he was elected President of the Senate, and when the Governor died in office, Baxter, by virtue of his position, succeeded to the governorship. Although some of the new Governor's policies were as conservative as those of the state he now headed, in many areas he was considered ahead of his time. Among other things, he advocated election reform, including women's suffrage; a public water storage system to be developed by the State; and the purchase by the State of burned or cut-over forest lands so that they might be reclaimed.

While still in the Legislature, Baxter had introduced a bill to create a state park and forest preserve in the Katahdin area. When it failed to pass, he reintroduced it in 1919. A second failure made it clear that he would need wider support for his plan, so he set about offsetting the resistance of the timber and water lobbies which, together with a general indifference, were his greatest sources of opposition. In 1920, he proposed the creation of a large Centennial State Park in recognition of a century of statehood. Naturally Baxter felt the park should be in the Katahdin area. In an attempt to gain support for his plan, he organized a well-publicized expedition of leading Republicans, newspaper editors and other citizens, which spent several days on the mountain. Again he failed but, tenacious if not downright stubborn, he continued the pursuit, even mentioning the Park concept in his farewell address as he left the governorship in 1925.

Baxter's nearest approach to success during those years was in 1921, when the Department of Inland Fisheries and Game established a 90,000-acre game preserve, a preserve encompassing most of the mountain. Three years later the Department constructed a cabin at Chimney Pond, and hired Mark LeRoy (Roy) Dudley as game warden. In one sense this move simply made official what Dudley had been

16

doing for several years. He had guided his first party to Katahdin when he was only eighteen, and by 1917 had built a three-man lean-to at Chimney Pond, which became known as Dudley's Den. Until his death in 1942, Dudley was instrumental in laying out and clearing some of the best-known trails on the mountain. However, he was probably most remembered for his highly imaginative tales of Indian spirits, especially the nasty-tempered Pamola.

Sometime during the five years after Baxter left office, when he realized that no amount of pressure from one public official was going to achieve the desired result, he decided to act as a private citizen. In 1930 he persuaded the Great Northern Paper Company to sell him a tract of 5,960 acres, which included most of Katahdin. The next year he deeded these lands to the state for use as a park, with the stipulation that the area "forever be used for public park and recreational purposes, forever left in the natural wild state, forever be kept as a sanctuary for wild beasts and birds, that no roads or ways for motor vehicles shall hereafter be constructed thereon or therein, and that I be allowed to retain, during my lifetime, the right to determine, and to place whatever markers or inscriptions shall be maintained or erected on or within the donated area herein offered to the State." The Legislature accepted the tract in the name of the people of the State of Maine, naming it Baxter State Park and renaming the highest peak of the Katahdin massif as Baxter Peak. Baxter continued to buy up parcels of land in the Katahdin area and deed them to the state. In 1939, one such gift alone tripled the size of the park, and it became obvious that what Baxter had in mind was almost breathtaking in scope. He had determined to increase the size of the park to as much as 200,000 acres, and to eventually provide financially for long-term operation. Meanwhile, to administer these magnificent gifts, the Legislature had created the Baxter State Park Commission in 1935, and in a reorganization in 1939, its members became the State Forest Commissioner, the Commissioner of Inland Fisheries and Game, and the Attorney General. Though the name was later changed to Baxter State Park Authority, the membership remains the same.

It was not easy for Baxter, even as a man of considerable wealth and prestige, to amass the huge acreage he needed to realize the dream. In buying up parcels from individual landowners and paper companies, for example, he found he had to make concessions that went against his policy of letting the land return to its wild state. In dealing with the paper companies he occasionally had to allow the

17

opening up of lumber roads and the cutting of timber in certain areas for specified periods of time. Acknowledging the enthusiasm for hunting on the part of citizens of communities adjacent to the Park, Baxter specifically excluded some of the Park lands from the game preserve, whose boundaries had become identical with those of the Park. In the case of sporting camps, leases were usually allowed to continue, although the land on which the camps stood was now owned by the State rather than by one of the paper companies or by private individuals. Whenever feasible, however, Baxter wanted the lands purchased for addition to the Park to return to the natural state as quickly as possible.

To prevent possible distortions or misinterpretations of his objectives, Baxter built several safeguards into his grants to the state. For instance, he stipulated that each gift of land be accepted by the Legislature separately, " . . . in the form of a separate State law carefully worded into a binding and unbreakable Trust Deed. In this manner a long list of precedents is being established; precedents which, as time passes, will show that eight or ten different Governors and as many Legislatures, by laws duly passed and signed by those Governors, have entered into solemn pacts that create a succession of irrevocable trusts." In 1955, at Baxter's request, the State Legislature passed an act which clarified the terms "Natural Wild State" and "Sanctuary for Wild Beasts and Birds." Five years later in a letter to Governor John Reed, he further defined his thoughts on the desired nature of the Park. With every additional gift of land, he reviewed the development of the Park to that point, and made new stipulations or modified old ones so that the Park would continue to develop along the lines he had envisioned. For example, in a conveyance in 1945, he restricted roads in the Park to the two in existence, the Millinocket-Sourdnahunk road approaching Katahdin from the south and west, and the Togue Pond-Roaring Brook road on the east. By 1949, however, he realized that these restrictions were too severe because they limited the number of people who could come to and enjoy the Park. Thus he gave the State the authority to construct such roads as would serve the people who wished to visit the Park, as long as they did not detract from "the natural wild state" of the region. In spite of these specific amendments, Baxter's major emphasis was on preservation of the wilderness. Although he wanted people to come to "his" park, to hike its trails and camp alongside the streams and ponds, he insisted that the "area is to be maintained primarily as a Wilderness, and recreational purposes are to be regarded as of secondary importance and shall not encroach upon the main objective of this area, which is to be 'forever wild'."

Until his last years, Baxter visited Katahdin every year to see that all was well with "this Park project [which] has become my life work." In addition he provided some funds for its operation, including the Baxter State Park Trust Fund, established in 1961, and finally a more than generous endowment upon his death in 1969. Since the establishment of the Park, new trails have been opened and new campgrounds developed. The staff of two part-time wardens who minded the Park in the 1930's has grown to thirteen permanent, and twenty-seven seasonal employees as of 1971. More than 65,000 people visited during that year, 45,000 of them spending at least one night there. Nevertheless, because of one man's perseverance, generosity, and foresight, Katahdin remains indomitable, its roots deep in the past, its peaks in the clouds.

Judith and John Hakola
Orono
March 1972

The literature on Katahdin is surprisingly vast, though much of it appears in publications not readily available to the general reader. Governor Percival P. Baxter's Papers, at the Maine State Library in Augusta, include much correspondence dealing with land acquisitions and park development and operation. For legislative and other legal aspects of the Katahdin area and Baxter State Park, see the laws of Maine in their various forms, and the records of debates in the Legislature for appropriate years.

Certain journals or publications are particularly important sources for material on Katahdin. Some of the more important articles are listed in this bibliography, but the files of the publications mentioned below should be consulted. *Appalachia,* the journal of the Appalachian Mountain Club, is particularly important since most issues have some mention of Katahdin. Of real importance for botanical information and trail histories for the twentieth century is *The Maine Naturalist. The Maine Sportsman* contains many articles on Katahdin and the surrounding region. For years the Great Northern Paper Company published *The Northern,* a valuable source of information on expeditions to the mountain, activities in the general area, and logging operations. For the first four decades of the twentieth century and more, the Bangor and Aroostook Railroad published a promotional journal, *In the Maine Woods.* This has become an invaluable source of articles and accounts of lumbering activities, river and lake expeditions, and the Katahdin area itself.

The basic bibliographical aid is *An Annotated Bibliography of Katahdin,* compiled by Edward S. C. Smith and Myron H. Avery, Publication No. 6, The Appalachian Trail Conference. This was first published in 1936, revised and corrected in 1937, and reprinted in 1950. It remains the most complete compilation of sources on Katahdin for the period prior to 1937, and is a must for anyone doing serious work on the mountain.

Some of the more important books and articles:

Appalachian Mountain Club. *Maine Mountain Guide.* 3rd ed. Boston: Appalachian Mountain Club, 1971. This contains descriptions of trails in Baxter State Park. Numerous versions of this guide have historical interest.

Avery, Myron H. "The Keep Path and its Successors—the History of Katahdin from the East and North." *Appalachia* XVII (December, 1928), 132-47, and (June, 1929) 224-37. As a major developer of the Appalachian Trail, Chairman of the

Appalachian Trail Conference, and the most important historian on Katahdin in the twentieth century, Avery constitutes an important source. He published widely in many journals.

"The Dead-Water Mountains." *The Maine Naturalist* X (March, 1930). Republished in abbreviated form in *In the Maine Woods*, 1933, 21-26.

"The Monument Line Surveyors on Katahdin." *Appalachia* XVII (June, 1928), 33-43.

Caldwell, Dabney W. *The Geology of Baxter State Park and Mt. Katahdin*. State Park Geologic Series #2 of Maine Geological Survey. Augusta, Maine: Department of Economic Development, 1960.

Douglas, William O. *My Wilderness: East to Katahdin*, 1961.

Eckstorm, Fannie H. *The Penobscot Man*, 1934. "The Katahdin Legends." *Appalachia* XVI (December, 1924), 39-52. This is probably the best explanation of the Katahdin Indian legends.

Hamlin, Charles E. "Routes to Ktaadn." *Appalachia* II (December, 1881), 306-31.

Higginson, Thomas Wentworth. "Going to Mount Katahdin." *Appalachia* XVI (June, 1925), 101-29. This description of an ascent made in 1855 first appeared in *Putnam's Monthly Magazine* for September, 1856.

Leavitt, H. Walter. *Katahdin Skylines*. Maine Technology Experiment Station, Paper No. 40. Orono, 1942. This was reprinted in 1954 and again in 1970. It is the most complete account of trail history and development in the twentieth century.

Maine Appalachian Trail Club, Incorporated. *Katahdin Section of Guide to the Appalachian Trail in Maine*. 6th ed. Washington, D.C.: The Appalachian Trail Confererence, 1965. This is a detailed description of roads and trails on and about Katahdin, and contains a good deal of historical information.

Smith, Marion Whitney. *Algonquian and Abenaki Indian Myths and Legends*. Lewiston, Maine: Central Maine Press, 1962.

Katahdin Fantasies. Augusta, Maine: K. J. Printing, 1953. These accounts must be used with great care.

Springer, John S. *Forest Life and Forest Trees*. Revised ed. Somersworth, New Hampshire: New Hampshire Publishing Company, 1971. Originally published in 1851, this remains a classic account of lumbering in Maine. Springer used some of the Reverend Marcus Keep's accounts for the section on Katahdin.

Thoreau, Henry D. *The Maine Woods*, var. eds. This classic and the chapter on "Ktaadn" have been reprinted many times.

Witherle, George H. "An Autumn Visit to the Sourdnahunk Mountains and Katahdin." *Appalachia* IV (December, 1884), 20-34.

"Explorations in the Vicinity of Mount Ktaadn." *Appalachia* V (June, 1888), 147-51.

"Explorations West and Northwest of Katahdin in the Late Nineteenth Century." Henry R. Buck and Myron H. Avery prepared (1928) this mimeographed summary of Witherle's explorations of the Katahdin area in the 1880's. It was reprinted by the Maine Appalachian Trail Club in 1950.

21

Greatest Mountain:

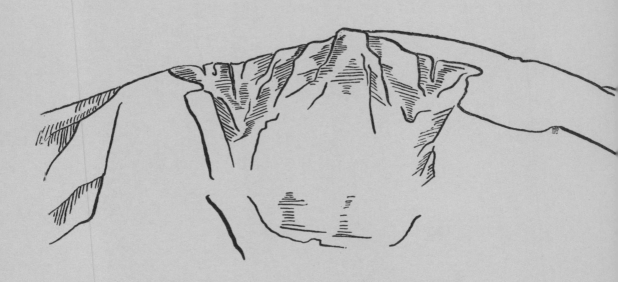

Katahdin's Wilderness

Excerpts from the writings of
Percival Proctor Baxter regarding his lifework
and photographs of
Katahdin His Eminence and the wild lands
below the summit by Constance Baxter

Everything in connection with the Park must be left simple and natural, and must remain as nearly as possible as it was when only the Indians and the animals roamed at will through these areas. I want it made available to persons of moderate means who, with their boys and girls, with their packs of bedding and food, can tramp through the woods, cook a steak and make flapjacks by the lakes and brooks. Every section of this area is beautiful, each in its own way. I do not want it locked up and made inaccessible; I want it used to the fullest extent but in the right, unspoiled way.

> *Communication*, to Governor H. A. Hildreth
> and the Ninety-second Legislature,
> Portland, Maine, January 2, 1945.

To most people Mount Katahdin is but a name. To those who have both seen and climbed the Mountain, it is a wonderful reality, and the memories of a trip to its summit remain vivid through the years. At present the great Mountain, weather-beaten by time and scarred by the avalanche, is almost inaccessible, the journey entailing expense, hardship and discomfort. The grandeur of the Mountain, its precipitous slopes, its massive cliffs, unusual formation and wonderful coloring cannot be surpassed or even equalled by any mountain east of the Mississippi river. Katahdin rises abruptly from the plain to the height of 5,273 feet, and, without foothills to detract from its solitary dignity, stands alone, a grim gray tower overlooking the surrounding country for hundreds of miles. It is small wonder that the aboriginal Indians believed it to be the home of the spirits of wind, storm and thunder.

From *Mount Katahdin State Park,* an
address to Maine Sportsmen's Fish
and Game Association, Augusta, Maine,
January 27, 1921.

The Knife-Edge

Pamola Peak and Knife-Edge

Pamola Peak in Winter

Katahdin always should and must remain the wild, storm-swept, untouched-by-man region it now is; that is its great charm. Only small cabins for mountain climbers and those who love the wilderness should be allowed there, only trails for those who travel on foot or horseback, a place where nature rules and where the creatures of the forest hold undisputed dominion.

From Portland Sunday *Telegram*, Portland, Maine, November 30, 1941.

Baxter Peak   *South Branch Pond*

Katahdin from the West

Cathedral Ridge

By day man stands spellbound in that solitude where man himself is an atom at the base of one of nature's noblest creations; by night he is inspired by the majesty of the moon as it rises and moves westward in a stately curve over the serrated peaks, which throw themselves up into the deep blue of the night as though to join the company of the stars.

The climb to Pamola Peak by a rough trail through stunted pine, over great granite boulders that lie spilled in endless drifts on the side of the Mountain . . .

From *Mount Katahdin State Park*

The Park stands right in the center of the northern portion of our State, a wild, mountainous country forever set aside and held in Trust by the State as a public park, forest reserve and wildlife sanctuary for present and future generations of Maine people . . . This district is typical of the wild lands of Maine. It has within its borders lakes, swamps, beaver dams, rivers, mountains, good timber lands and burnt-over lands, meadows and boulders in profusion. Moose, deer, wildcats, bears, foxes and all the smaller animals and birds abound therein. All these creatures are safe from the hunters, and the sound of the axe and of falling trees never will echo through these forests.

From Portland Sunday *Telegram.*

The history of these lands is fascinating. It is a story of violent speculation in which fortunes were lost and men's reputations ruined, and in which fortunes were won and great timber-owning families were established, and made wealthy for generations to come. It is a story of intrigue and corruption, where powerful and selfish men often took that to which they had no right, from those too weak to defend themselves and their property. It is a story in which the rights of the people in a princely inheritance were given away or bartered for a song, for the folly of which future generations forever will pay.

From *Mount Katahdin State Park*

Katahdin from Stacyville

With the protection of wildlife, the deer, the moose and the birds no longer will fear man and gradually they will come out of their forest retreats and show themselves. I want hunting with cameras to take the place of hunting with guns. Aircraft frighten wildlife and disturb the peace and solitude of the wilderness. Would that the day may come when all of Maine will become a sanctuary for the beasts and birds of the forest and field, and when cruelty to the humbler orders of life no longer stalks the land.

Communication, to the Governor and the Ninety-second Legislature.

Twenty-six years ago, when I first conceived the idea of a State Park at Katahdin, there was determined opposition. I was attacked as a dreamer and branded as a socialist. Several of our newspapers came out against me: "We don't want a Park, leave things as they are; what shall we do with it?" again was heard. Session after session I fought on and made speech after speech, up and down the State. It was a long road to travel, but today the State Park is acknowledged to be one of the State's great natural attractions and the people of the future will appreciate it even more than do those of today.

Communication, to Governor S. Sewall
and the Ninety-first Legislature,
Portland, Maine, January 13, 1943.

In 1917, I first proposed that the State make a beginning in creating a Park at Katahdin. From that date until now I have worked diligently and patiently upon this project and have seen it grow from small beginnings to its present ample proportions. In the years to come, when the Forests of our State have been cut off and disappeared, when civilization has encroached upon the land we now refer to as "Wild Land," this Park will give the people of succeeding generations a living example of what the State of Maine was "in the good old days," before the song of the woodsman's axe and the whine of the power saw was heard in the land. I am confident that the people of Maine, as time passes, will appreciate this Park and that the State never will break these Trusts. I know the conscience and the Soul of Maine. The word of this State as given in Acts passed by its Legislatures and signed by its Governors is as sacred a pledge and trust as Man can make.

> *Communication*, to Governor E. S. Muskie
> and the Ninety-seventh Legislature,
> Portland, Maine, January 11, 1955.

There are several approaches to the Mountain, but the most picturesque is that which leads from the East into the South Basin, where is located Chimney Pond, a beautiful sheet of water, which, among ponds, is as unique in its coloring and setting as Katahdin is among its sister mountains. This pond is surrounded on the South and West by a grand amphitheatre of perpendicular cliffs rising from 1500 to 2000 feet. The water in this remarkable pond is so clear and cold that fish cannot live in it, and it is as uninhabited as the salt brine of the Dead Sea. Its surface mirrors the ever-changing aspects of the clouds and the multi colored cliffs towering around it. These cliffs are gray, blue, pink, or brown, according as the atmosphere changes from hour to hour, or as the position of the sun is altered.

From *Mount Katahdin State Park*

Chimney Pond from the East Face

I want no hard-surfaced roads in this Park, my object being to have it remain as nearly as possible in its natural wild state, unimproved by man.

Communication, to the Governor and the Ninety-second Legislature.

As modern civilization with its trailers and gasoline fumes, its unsightly billboards, its radio and jazz, encroaches on the Maine wilderness, the time yet may come when only the Katahdin region remains undefiled by man.

From Portland Sunday *Telegram*

I want pleasant foot-trails built and attractive campsites laid out in the valleys, by the brooks and on the shores of the waters. Sites where simple forest lean-tos and small log cabins are available for those who love nature and are willing to walk and make an effort to get close to nature.

Communication, to the Governor and
the Ninety-second Legislature.

When you inspect this map it will be difficult for you to visualize how this has been accomplished, how my numerous purchases have been brought together into one solid area. I myself can hardly realize it. A map showing the different acquisitions, both small and large, over the years, would remind you of your grandmother's patchwork quilt which finally, in some mysterious way, came out of the confusion into one large piece.

Communication, to the Governor and
the Ninety-seventh Legislature,
Portland, Maine, March 17, 1955.

Mouse-munched mushroom

Having in mind the fact that the people of Maine once owned these great areas of timberland, is it not fitting that, upon payment of a fair price therefor, the grandest and most beautiful portion of all this great area which the people of the State once possessed, should again become their property?

From *Mount Katahdin State Park*

I will never forget the thrill I received the day I met the officials of the Great Northern Paper Company and received from them the deed to the mountain I had purchased. It had taken me twenty-eight years to obtain the first 6,000 acres on the mountain, but it was worth it.

From Bangor Daily *News*,
Bangor, Maine, May 3, 1938.

Katahdin over Togue Pond

After consulting with several of the leading judges and lawyers of our State, a definite plan has been adopted under which I am to deed a considerable area to the State at each Legislative Session, each deed to be accepted in the form of a separate State law carefully worded into a binding and unbreakable Trust Deed. In this manner a long list of precedents is being established; precedents which, as time passes, will show that eight or ten different Governors and as many Legislatures, by laws duly passed and signed by these Governors, have entered into solemn pacts that create a succession of irrevocable trusts. These trusts, beginning with 1931, are printed in the Laws of Maine, and as each session enacts them they thus become public documents.

Communication, to Governor S. Sewall
and the Ninetieth Legislature,
Portland, Maine, January 12, 1942.

In all the deeds from me to the State, the phrases "natural wild state" and "as a sanctuary for wild beasts and birds" have been used. By these I do not intend that the Park forever shall be a region unvisited and neglected by man. I seek to provide against commercial exploitation, against hunting, trapping and killing, against lumbering, hotels, advertising, hot-dog stands, motor vehicles, horse-drawn vehicles and other vehicles, aircraft, and the trappings of unpleasant civilization. Nor is the Park to be kept exclusively for professional mountain climbers; it is for everybody.

Communication, to the Governor and the Ninety-second Legislature.

As to roads within the Park, this must be left to the discretion of the Park Authority, but I request that no additional roads for automobiles be constructed therein and that no additional camps be erected such as those at Katahdin Stream, Abol, Trout Brook, Roaring Brook, Sourdnahunk Stream, Chimney Pond and Russell Pond.

Letter, to Governor J. H. Reed
and Members of the Executive Council,
Portland, Maine, May 20, 1960.

While I am living, I fear no encroachments on the Park, but as time passes and new men appear upon the scene, there may be a tendency to overlook these restrictions and thus break the spirit of these gifts.

Letter, to the Governor and
Members of the Executive Council.

This area is to be maintained primarily as a wilderness, and recreational purposes are to be regarded as of secondary importance and shall not encroach upon the main objective of this area, which is to be "forever wild."

From Portland Evening *Express*, Portland, Maine, June 20, 1957.

Certainly he is a bold and reckless person who, even after I have deceased, attempts to induce this State to violate the Trust provisions created under a long series of Deeds and Acts of Acceptance extending from 1931 almost until 1950.

Communication, to the Governor and the Ninety-first Legislature.

Katahdin over the West Branch of the Penobscot River

The great plateau extends for miles from the South Peak to the North Peak. It is wind-swept and strewn with huge granite boulders that seem to have been shaken from the clouds by a giant hand. It is covered in places with a dense growth of knee-high scrub spruce and pine, through which it is impossible for man to pass. This plateau once was the home of a large herd of caribou, all of which were killed or driven northward by the relentless hunter. I have talked with woodsmen who distinctly remember these strange animals as they grazed over this elevated feeding ground, or stood on the edge of the Mountain looking over into the great space beyond.

From *Mount Katahdin State Park*

The Katahdinauguoh from the Summit Plateau

Human life is both short and uncertain. This being so, I wish to have this Park completed during my lifetime, in so far as I am able. When the land is accepted by the State during my lifetime I know it is accepted properly and for all time. My executors thereby are spared the details of this work, with which they would not be familiar.

Communication, to the Governor and the Ninety-second Legislature.

Maine is famous for its 2500 miles of seacoast, with its countless islands, for its myriad lakes and ponds, and for its forests and rivers, but Mount Katahdin Park will be the State's crowning glory, a worthy memorial to commemorate the end of the first and the beginning of the second century of Maine's statehood. This park will prove a blessing to those who follow us, and they will see that we built for them more wisely than our forefathers did for us. Shall any great timberland or paper-making corporation, or group of such corporations, themselves the owners of millions of acres of Maine forests, say to the People of this State, "You shall not have Mount Katahdin, either as a memorial of your past or as a heritage for your future"?

From *Mount Katahdin State Park*,
the concluding paragraph.

Afterword

The Katahdin Trust was created when Percival Baxter gave the people of the State of Maine 200,000 acres to be used "for a state forest, public park and recreational purposes ... forever to be left in the natural wild state and ... forever kept as a sanctuary for wild beasts and birds ... "

Over a period of thirty years former Governor Baxter purchased, and subsequently bequeathed in trust, parcels of land around and including Mount Katahdin. The 200,000 acres bear the name Baxter State Park, perhaps an unfortunate name in these times because the Park is often equated with other parks in the Maine State Park system which differ radically in their intent and administration. Baxter wanted the Katahdin wilderness area known as a *State Park* in order to distinguish it from *National Park* — to show clearly that the Park belonged to the people of Maine. In the early 1930's there was pressure to open up the Katahdin area and make it into a National Park. Baxter refused vehemently, as he was opposed to the commercial exploitation which would probably have accompanied such a change. Since a similar threat no longer exists, and since the name "State Park" is detrimental to the Park if it is to function as a wilderness preserve, it is now referred to by many as *Baxter Wilderness Park*.

At first glance, it may seem that in the various Deeds of Trust, Baxter built in a dilemma which could in time mean the demise of wilderness in the Park. In other words, public recreation in the modern sense and the "forever wild" concept are diametrically opposed. But if one examines the writings closely, one can understand that it was not recreation in today's sense that was meant. Baxter wanted Man to enjoy the area, but without dragging along the endless paraphernalia of technological civilization. Thus, the only way for the area to remain essentially as it was during Indian habitation would be for

Man to return simply and humbly. And on this score, for many years the administration of Baxter Wilderness Park has stood alone, a bulwark against exploitation of the Park. There is a reservations system, there are dirt roads, chemical toilets, and no souvenir stands. It was not until recently, however, that tight vehicular control had to be clamped on the Park for, until the advent of the camper, trailer, and snowmobile era, Man and this wilderness park were not at odds. It became evident, however, that the machines were very detrimental, and they were ordered out. Campers, trailers, trail bikes, and motorcycles are not allowed through the gates. Snowmobiles are allowed on the perimeter road only, to be used for transportation, *not recreation*. Man is thus being forced to come into these wilds simply, and if he is unable to do so, he should go elsewhere.

As to the photography, I have many mixed emotions concerning Katahdin's wilderness. I had returned to Maine after a six-year absence and it felt good. I lived beautifully in a small cabin built over the waters of Millinocket Lake, which served as my bathtub, supplied dishwater, and afforded me a full view of His Eminence from my pillow. Here I resided with a friend acquired specifically for the purpose; Angel, a Lab-Dane cross. Plus a few books and a chessboard.

And so I wandered with the camera, alone and with friends. I watched the seasons come and go on the calendar of the flora; the fresh, startling greens of spring, the wildflowers and fruits of summer, the berries and mushrooms of August, the astounding fall with its forests of ethereal colors — and winter, with quiet and soft whiteness. Each month, each season more beautiful than the last, until I realized that it's all fantastic. Except, of course, the black flies, mosquitoes, and humidity. I remember walking eleven and a half miles from South Branch to Russell Pond (two miles over the usual due to an ambiguously marked trail) on a July day during a heat wave in which the air had not moved for ten days, with eighty-five percent humidity, black flies and mosquitoes ever-present, and the canopy of green leaves suffocating. At that point, I had a tough time convincing myself I was fond of the Maine woods.

On the other hand, my first ascent of Mount Katahdin (since childhood) started with a June storm in the air. The clouds came and went as we climbed Cathedral Ridge, and as we reached Chimney Peak the storm broke upon us with thunder, lightning, and rain. Warm rain, and I reveled in the whole spectacle in spite of the danger. It was glorious. As was the February storm which marooned our party of four on the summit ridge for an extra night. When prepared, a battle with the elements is exhilarating.

But then I remember standing on the edge of Chimney Pond in late June photographing the setting sunlight on the rock wall. I wore a beehive hat, to no avail, and my pants and vest were black with black flies. They were in my eyebrows, hair, mouth. It was a torturous half hour, an attempt to endure and maintain some semblance of sanity. I managed, primarily by telling myself that the experience would have a purging effect, that I would have a new lease on life if I successfully ignored the damned things. Nevertheless, there were many months of relaxed, bug-free photography. In August, for instance, when I walked through the woods and every few feet found a different mushroom shouting brilliant colors. I would crouch and examine it, put the extension tube on the camera, then get into an eye-level position, flat on my stomach with my chin resting in the dirt. There I would lie watching the light come and go as the slight wind blew the leaves into and out of interference with the sun. Each of the mushrooms is unique and short-lived, and on more than one occasion I returned a day later to pay my regards, only to find my friend either entirely missing or else the remnants shriveled and brown. Such experiences make one thankful for happening along at the right time, but also make one wonder what was missed.

So, although I got lonely living alone, I shall think back fondly on my cabin, my communion with the smaller forms of life, the Mountain, the seasons, the exertion, all the things and people that went into making this work on Baxter Wilderness Park a rewarding one. And to those who helped in so many ways, my appreciation and affection: Pepi Stiegler, who accompanied me several times to the summit, twice to the interior, waited for me sometimes and takes care of me most times. My grandfather, John Baxter, for his support and our occasional rendezvous over lobster dinner. Dorothy Shorey, and Barbara and Ryan Fendler for their generosity in providing friendship and a home away from home. Jane Fuller, Mary Ann and Tim Dunn, Joanne Kornick, Andi and Eric Gladstone Burton, Nick Danforth, and George Smith and the nine other Yetis of the winter expedition, all of whom gave me company which I needed because it gets scary up there in them woods. The Baxter State Park Authority and Advisory Committee for permissions granted, and for their concerted efforts on behalf of the wilderness in Baxter Wilderness Park. Josepha Haveman, for the use of her studio and darkroom in Berkeley during preparation of the book. And Dave Bohn, for energies spent on my photography and the design of this book, whose ability to teach and inspire has formed a broad basis in the medium I plan to make my life's work, and the germination of whose ideas always manages to result in beautiful work.

And mostly, Percival Proctor Baxter, for the incredible foresight.

Constance Baxter
Berkeley
February 1972

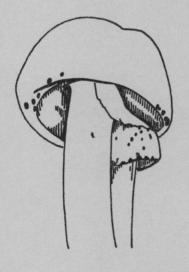

This book was printed in an edition of five thousand copies by Noel Young Press, Santa Barbara, for the letterpress text sections, and by Rood Associates, Santa Barbara, for the black and white and four-color lithography. The paper is Simpson Lee Corsican; sand, rust, and white. Typeface is Trump Mediaeval. Composition and title page design by Graham Mackintosh Seven hundred-fifty copies were hand-bound in linen by Earle Gray of Los Angeles Presswork by Jim Jimenez and Richard Ulin. Production by Richard Schuettge. Designed and edited by Dave Bohn

Katahdin   he different

mountain once was man